ROCKFORD PUBLIC LIBRARY

3 1112 01478018 9

W9-BJL-529

J 551.43 GIL
Gill, Shelley
Up on Denali : Alaska's
wild mountain

081406

WITHDRAWN

ROCKFORD PUBLIC LIBRARY

Rockford, Illinois

www.rockfordpubliclibrary.org

815-965-9511

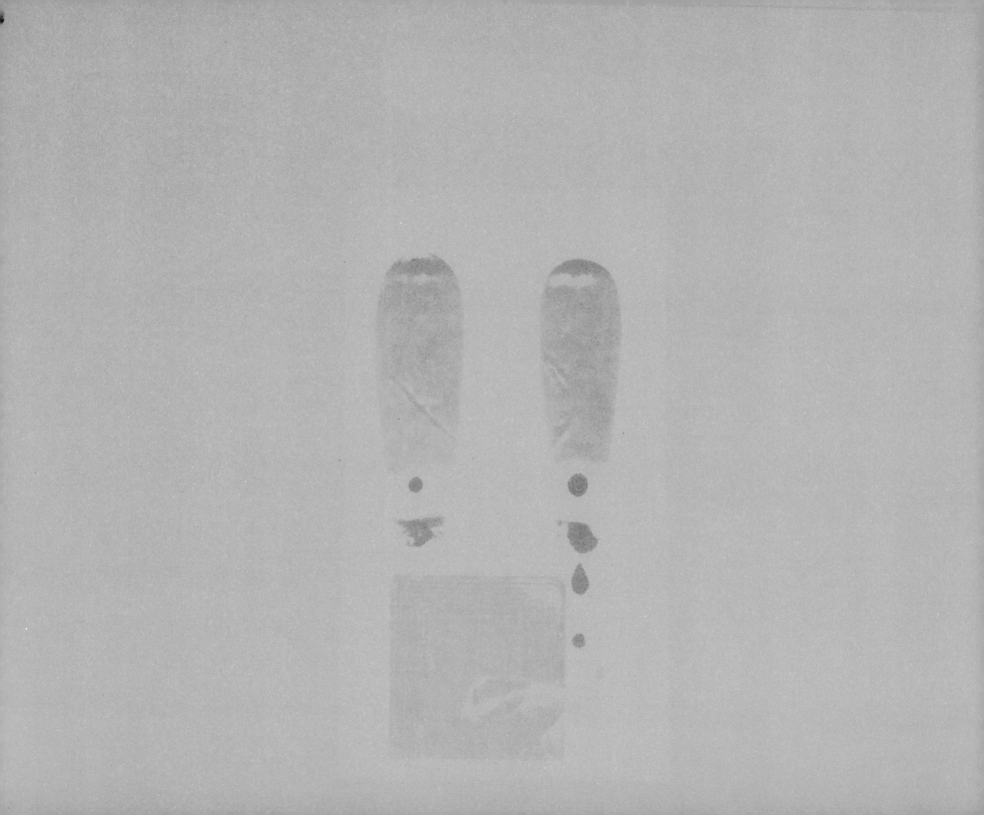

Up on Denali

SHELLEY GILL

Illustrated by
SHANNON CARTWRIGHT

PAWS IV published by
SASQUATCH BOOKS
WWW.SASQUATCHBOOKS.COM

ROCKFORD PUBLIC LIBRARY

Up on Denali

Text ©2006 Shelley Erskine Gill

Illustrations ©2006 by Shannon Cartwright

All rights reserved. No portion of this book may be reproduced or utilized in any form, or by any electronic, mechanical, or other means without the prior written permission of the publisher.

Printed in China

Published by Sasquatch Books

Distributed by Publishers Group West

17 16 15 14 13 12 11 10 09 08 07 06   8 7 6 5 4 3 2 1

Library of Congress Cataloging-in-Publication Data

Gill, Shelley.

     Up on Denali : Alaska's wild mountain / by Shelley Gill ; illustrations by Shannon Cartwright.

p. cm.

ISBN 1-57061-366-4 — ISBN 1-57061-365-6 (pbk)

1. McKinley, Mount (Alaska)—Juvenile literature. 2. Mountains—Alaska—Juvenile literature.

  3. Athapascan mythology—Juvenile literature. I. Cartwright, Shannon, ill. II. Title.

GB525.5.A4G55 2006   551.43'09798'3—dc22   2005051507

Sasquatch Books

119 South Main Street, Suite 400 / Seattle, WA 98104

(206) 467-4300 / www.sasquatchbooks.com / custserv@sasquatchbooks.com

To Shannon Cartwright, in celebration of 25 years of collaboration with the best illustrator ever. And to our readers, in the hope you will cherish this amazing place called Alaska.
Many thanks to Denali education specialist Howard Carbone, Denali geologist Phil Brease, and Alaskan climber and guide Brian Okonek. —S.G.

To Wendy: Thank you for sharing your creativity and your love of children's books. Also, a special thank you to Marge Nord. —S.C.

When the snow starts to snow and the winds really blow, Raven comes out to play. Other birds have gone south but curious old raven can endure the long, cold arctic winters. He is a genius of birds, creative, inquisitive, and a THIEF!

View of Denali from the North

Denali/Mt. McKinley
South Peak
20,320 ft.
North Peak
19,470 ft.

Mt. Deception
11,826 ft.

Mt. Brooks
11,940 ft.

Mt. Silverthrone
13,220 ft.

Mt. Tatum
11,140 ft.

Mt. Carpe
12,550 ft.

View of Denali from the South

Denali/Mt. McKinley
South Peak
North Peak

Mt. Foraker
17,400 ft.

Mt. Hunter
14,573 ft.

Moose's Tooth
10,335 ft.

3

In the heart of Alaska there's a mountain that rises so high it creates its own weather. It is one of the coldest mountains on planet earth. This mountain has many names: McKinley, Denali, the Big One, the High One, and simply, the Mountain. Huge glaciers slide from the mountain's shoulders, giving way to white-water rivers. Wildflowers blanket the tundra for only a few short months before winter covers the land in ice and snow. This is a wild mountain: one face a paradise, the other face lifeless, locked in deadly ice.

How did Denali come to be? The Athabascan Indians tell a creation story: Raven Man was chasing a girl. But he wasn't having much luck. Peeved at her lack of affection he threw her from his canoe. Whew, was her mom mad! She set two grizzlies on Raven. He paddled as fast as he could as the bears dug at the lake's edge and raised huge waves that threatened to tip Raven from his canoe.

Raven hurled his harpoon at the waves. It glanced off the first and lodged in the second, larger wave. The waves turned to stone—the first one became a set of low hills, the second a great mountain called Deenaalee. And Raven, that trickster, got clean away.

The Athabascan Indians who lived near Denali were tough nomadic hunters who could survive at temperatures of 50 below for days without food, fire, or shelter.

7

68–82 million
years ago

Dinosaur fossils 68–82 million years old have been found north and southeast of Denali and in the park.

**Volcanic rainbow bands
paint the hills of Polychrome Pass.
Glaciers grind and echo
songs of mountain and crevasse.**

In the language of science the birth of Denali happened another way. Think of two giant hunks of land smashing together under terrific force. Edges fold, huge cracks appear, heat melts the stone to liquid. Sand is pressed to stone, twisting, crunching, thrusting upward as one hunk pushes the other toward the sky.

Denali is unique in that it is made up of many different terrains deposited over millions of years. Remnants of ocean bottom can be found high in the Alaska Range—some from exotic South Pacific origins. An uplifted mountain, Denali rises higher as the North American and Pacific plates of earth's crust collide and one slides under the other. This mountain uplifting continues today. Denali grows about one millimeter a year!

As the mountains build they are also constantly worn away. More recent chiseling of the land was done by ice and water. The V-shaped valleys were carved by the water of raging rivers.

Series of glaciations over the last 2.5 million years until present.

About 1.8 million years ago a whole slew of prehistoric critters showed up just north of Denali.

When the first humans appeared near Denali about 11,000 years ago, the prehistoric mammal population began to decline.

The U-shaped valleys were carved by the ice of grinding glaciers.

9

At the feet of Wild Mountain,
trumpeter swans call.
Lynx, moose, and black bear
sing a melody of fall.

Redpole

Wilson's Warbler

Hawk Owl

Marten

Porcupine

Magpie

Moose

Beaver

Fireweed

River Otter

Redbreasted Merganser

Common Loon

Mew Gull

Goshawk

Golden Eagle

Common Raven

Spruce Grouse

Grizzly Bear

Black Bear

Wolf

Coyote

Red Fox

Snowshoe Hare

Wild Mountain wiggles his toes in the cool lowlands and shadows of a spruce forest. Moose and caribou with huge racks and big grizzlies with waves of fat beneath golden fur live and play at the feet of Wild Mountain. Black bear, lynx, marten, grizzly, and moose live along the river drainages that flow from glaciers high above. Many of those rivers—Kahiltna, Tokositna, Yentna, Chulitna, Kantishna— end in "na," Athabascan for "running water."

On a hot day the glaciers melt faster and the rivers run high, but as the weather cools the water slows and drops its load of silt. This changes the course of the rivers as they meander through the lowlands.

Whistling Swan

Lynx

Least Weasel

Muskrat

Wolverine

11

At the knees of Wild Mountain see the tundra in full bloom, buttercups and shooting stars, bluebells and pink plumes.

Northern Wheatear

Climbing up through tundra is like walking through a rainbow of wildflowers. But not all the flowers on the mountain have pretty names. In fact, some are pretty strange: toadflax, woolly lousewort, wormwood, fleabane, duckweed, or how about . . . weasel snout!

Frigid Arnica

Weasel Snout

Woolly Lousewort

Marmots

Dwarf Dogwood

Forget-me-not

Snow Buttercup

Moss Campion

Mountain Harebell

Frigid Shooting Star

Mountain Aven

Yellow Violet

In this tiny three-inch jungle of tundra, windflowers sway along a steep streambed. An antler lies buried in moss, and the ground is a spongy mattress beneath your feet. Clumps of color—magenta, sky blue, waxy yellow—sprout from rocky faces. Willow whiskers poke through pockets of dirty old snow.

Dall Sheep

Alaska Poppy

Siberian Aster

Rosewort

Pink Plume

Dwarf Fireweed   Heather   Wild Geranium   Twin Flower   Bear Flower   Bluebell   Prickly Rose   Collared Pika

13

Arctic Tern

**Bearberries stored in tundra nest,
grayling eggs hidden in gravel.
Arctic tern takes his northern rest
as 'round the world he'll travel.**

Cranberries, blueberries, crowberries, cloudberries. YUM!
Food is everywhere if you're a bear! Clear lakes and
ponds are home to Dolly Varden, trout, salmon, grayling,
sticklebacks, wood frogs, leeches, and MOSQUITOES! The
tundra wetlands are nesting grounds for shorebirds
and provide a resting place for the migrating birds
whose destination is
farther north.

Snow Bunting

Cranberry

Bog Blueberry

Vole

Crowberry

Cloudberry

Alaska State Bird

Whimbrel

Large-billed Dowitcher

Solitary Sandpiper

Lesser Yellowlegs

Long-tailed Jaeger

Ground Squirrel

Alpine Bearberry

Wood Frog   Rock Ptarmigan

15

Trout   Stickleback   Grayling   Dolly Varden

Scats, turds, and pellets
can give a kid the scoop.
No matter what you call it,
you can learn a lot from poop!

Currants

Hiking the tundra, you can learn a lot about an animal's habits by studying scat. You can find out what critters are up to and maybe figure out when the grizzly left that steamy pile of poo behind your tent. You can even tell if a bear is eating soapberries because his poop will be pink.

Hmm . . . what happens when bears eat blueberries?

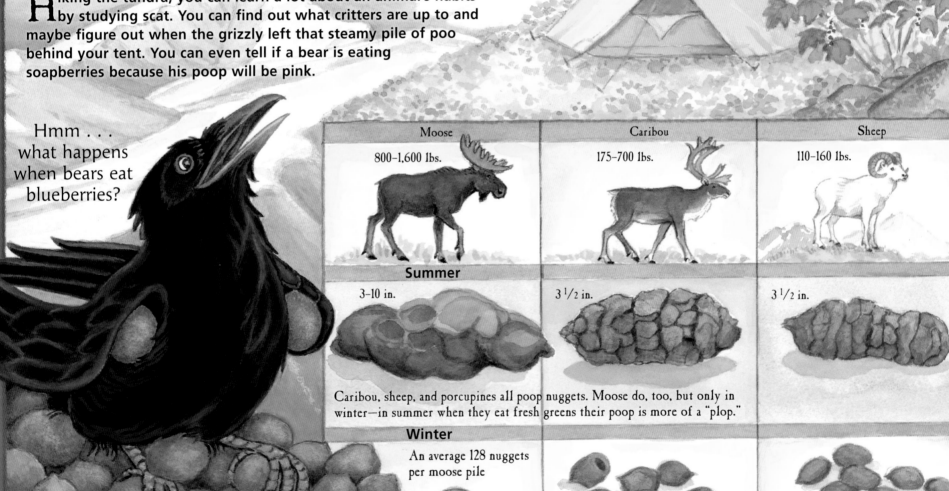

Moose	Caribou	Sheep
800–1,600 lbs.	175–700 lbs.	110–160 lbs.

Summer

3–10 in.	3 1/2 in.	3 1/2 in.

Caribou, sheep, and porcupines all poop nuggets. Moose do, too, but only in winter—in summer when they eat fresh greens their poop is more of a "plop."

Winter

An average 128 nuggets per moose pile

16

Soapberry

Wolf

89–120 lbs.

6 1/4 in.

Porcupine

15–40 lbs.

Pika

4–8 oz.

Ptarmigan

Overnight nest

You can tell if the ground squirrel is out of hibernation if his bones are in a fox's scat.

**Awesome antlers, heavy horns
impress a critter's mates,
in a clashing, crashing contest
to see who can get the most dates.**

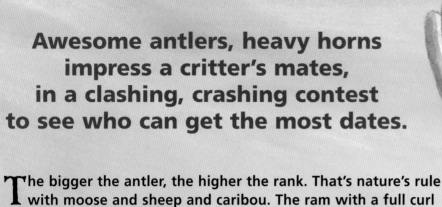

The bigger the antler, the higher the rank. That's nature's rule with moose and sheep and caribou. The ram with a full curl headset is more successful with the gals. He will breed more often and pass on his mega genes.

Antlers start growing in early spring and are covered with brown fuzzy hair called velvet.

They grow all summer and die in the early fall. The bulls scrape the velvet off by thrashing their antlers against bushes and trees. For a few days the antlers are blood red with exposed blood vessels.

18

Dall sheep—both the ewes and rams—grow permanent horns that get a little bigger each year. Horn is made from keratin, like your fingernails and hair. Male moose and caribou couples grow antlers that are shed each year. Next year the new antler grows a little thicker. A mature bull moose can have antlers weighing in at 90 pounds! Antlers are made from bone.

Horns on sheep
they always keep;
Antlers on moose
each winter
come loose!

The antlers harden as winter approaches. They turn to brown bone and after a few weeks bleach ivory in the sun.

Antlers fall off in the winter. All these steps are controlled by the amount of daylight. The antlers are yummy treats gnawed on by lots of critters for extra calcium!

Porcupine 3 in. long

Lynx 3 ½ in. long

Marmot 2 ½ in. long

Beaver 5 in. long

**Bear blaze, caribou rack.
Eagle talon, wolf track.
Postholes tell of a moose alone.
Wolverine guards his pile of bone.**

Huge bear tracks cover the rounded cut left by the caribou's hoof in the sand of a dry riverbed. There is a story here and the ending lies close by. Wolf, fox, and eagle tracks crisscross a scant pile of bones—two hooves, a clump of hair—all that remain of the young bull caribou. The bear killed the caribou but the leftovers fed many.

A "bear blaze" is where a big bear rubs a tree's bark off at the top of his reach. This may be a warning to other bears.

Grizzly front paw 5 ½ in. long

Wolf 4 ¾ in. long

Wolverine 4 ½ in. long

Fox 2 ½ in. long

Ground Squirrel
1 in. long

Pika
½ in. long

Raven
3 ½ in. long

Do you know why bear tracks
are bigger in the fall?
(Because the bear weighs more.)

*When you see
caribou tracks in
the snowy cleft of
a mountain, what
do they tell you?*

*Maybe . . .
the bugs are out!
Clouds of black flies,
gnats, and mosquitoes
evaporate on the cold
wind skimming across a left-
over snowfield. The bugs in
Alaska are so hungry they can
suck a young animal dry. So caribou
stick to the cool, less buggy snowfields—especially when they have
their calves.*

Weasel
½ in. long

Eagle 6 in. long

Sheep 3 in. long

Moose 6 in. long

Caribou
5 in. long

21

Harsh exposed ridge
windwhipped, bone dry.
A bunny's gotta boogie
if he's gonna survive.

A blanket of
tundra barely covers
Wild Mountain's belly. Small
isolated patches of vegetation
provide shelter for a few hardy mountain
folk. On the north fork of the Ruth Glacier,
surrounded by snow, a family of carnivorous bunnies
lives at the base of a glacier ridge. Pikas—known as rock rabbits—
usually gather plants, dry them in the sun, and store this "hay" for
winter. But biologists have noted meat-eating pikas in the Wrangell
Mountains and suspect they are doing the same on Denali.

In the Wrangells, scientists found caches of small
birds "stacked like cordwood" in pika nests.
A meat-eating rabbit.
Yikes!

A colony of gray-crowned rosy finches have been seen nesting in cliffs at 7,200-foot Kahiltna base camp. They survive and raise their young by collecting insects blown up the face of the glacier.

19,240 ft. North Peak

17,400 ft. freezing temperatures year round; only lichens live here

15,500 ft. a tuft of grass

12,500 ft. melting occurs to this point

6,000–7,000 ft. microclimates where just a few plants grow among the sun-warmed rocks

5,000–6,000 ft. mosses end

5,000 ft. most vegetation ends

2,700 ft. tree line

23

The crack of blue ice,
an avalanche roars by.
Glacier grinds forward
with a haunting cry.

Denali is surrounded by huge
glaciers and ice fields. On the south
slope the Kahiltna, Tokasitna, Ruth, and Eldridge,
and on the north slope the Muldrow and Brooks flow downhill, pushed
by the weight of accumulated snow. The Alaska Range acts as a barrier
to the storms moving in from the Pacific Ocean so the moisture
dumps on the south slope as snow, creating the south slope's
huge snowfields and glaciers. The rivers of ice surge and
retreat, and as the ice moves it cracks—leaving deep and
dangerous crevasses. These 100- to 300-feet-deep cracks
look beautiful from the air, but they are deadly.

In summer a red-pigmented
algae can grow on the snow,
turning it a pale pink.

Park Service volunteers were struggling through deep drifts at 13,500 feet when they saw a grizzly bear emerge from the blowing snow. At the sight of the humans the bear bolted back down the mountain and slipped, tumbling into a crevasse. The mountain claimed another victim.

Glaciers can also be a death trap for many migrating birds that follow the wide valley north, only to find a giant mountain blocking their path. Sparrows, dark-eyed juncos, warblers, ducks, and geese have tried to take this shortcut and ended up buried in the ice. But the strangest animal story yet is the sighting of a red squirrel at 12,500 feet—10,000 feet above the last tree. Did he travel up in a climber's pack or just get lost?

Glacier streams are a soupy gray because of the silt—rock ground to powder by the movement of the ice.

Erratics are huge boulders left in odd places when the river of ice moving them along recedes.

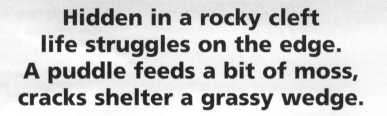

Hidden in a rocky cleft
life struggles on the edge.
A puddle feeds a bit of moss,
cracks shelter a grassy wedge.

On the shoulders of Wild Mountain, crisp dry lichens go slimy in freezing rain. A small patch of grass is found at 15,000 feet, a bit of moss grows in a crevice at 17,500 feet. The rest of the view is rock and ice.

But somehow tiny microclimates hang on in rock cracks where water can collect—a puddle forms and lichen grows. At 12,000 feet the temperature rarely gets above freezing. The air is thinner and the wind is stronger. Yet these miniature islands of life cling to south-facing slopes. At 5,000 feet patches of willow, lousewort, and saxifrage survive.

Year after year a pilot has seen wolverine tracks climbing the Straightaway Glacier in the spring, to the Sultana Ridge of Mount Foraker to more than 13,000 feet, then descending Mount Crosson, down the Kahiltna, and out Pika Glacier. The wolverine is migrating across the highest part of the Alaska Range—to the south in the summer and back north in the winter.

Climber and naturalist Brian Okonek was climbing in a whiteout at 9,000 feet when he came upon a flock of eight shorebirds flying in V formation . . . going nowhere. They were just staying even with the headwind—flapping but not moving forward as Brian walked by.

At 9,500 feet on Kahiltna Pass climbers saw a raven chasing a duck—staying right on his tail—with a hungry look in his eye.

Icy pinnacles sweep the sky.
Above the clouds I long to fly.
To seek, to climb, to explore;
Mountain, teach my heart to soar.

The High One. Rising 18,000 feet from its 2,000-foot plateau, Denali's face is higher even than Everest's. The mountain sits in the center of the Alaska Range, craggy white slopes blushing pink in winter's alpenglow. It has been called the coldest mountain in the world with winds up to 150 mph and temperatures that plummet to 200 below.

Frederick Cook claimed he climbed Denali first, but later photos showed he had a flair for fiction. Two local miners with the Sourdough Expedition did climb the North Peak in 1910. They traveled—first with horses and later with dog teams—150 roadless miles from Fairbanks and then climbed the mountain without ropes, hauling a 14-foot spruce pole from which they hoisted Old Glory.

28

Each year hundreds of climbers from around the world strike out from Kahiltna base camp at 7,200 feet. From there they ferry their supplies up 17 miles to a series of higher camps before attempting the summit. They try and avoid plunging in crevasses, being buried by avalanches, falling ill to altitude sickness, freezing to death, and simply blowing off the mountain. Most make it. Some don't.

Kahiltna Base Camp

The best time to climb is April to June when the weather has calmed down and the snow is still stable.

At the crown of Wild Mountain
a raven streaks by,
diving on wind currents
that twist in the sky.

Climbers struggle to the summit to spend a few moments marveling at the beauty beneath their feet. Ravens, on the other hand, play tag here. They are the spirit of Denali, looping and twisting in ravaging storms, searching for a treasure of oatmeal and powdered soup. Screaming their raspy *haw caw* as they dive-bomb the hapless humans.

Lenticular dish-shaped clouds above the summit signal bad weather is on the way.

100 million years ago the dark loose rocks found today at the summit of Denali were part of a sea floor.

Climbers and ravens play a game. At the moment humans are ahead. The climbers once used bamboo wands to mark their food caches up and down the mountain. Ravens learned to look for the bamboo wands as markers to dig for their next meal. So climbers no longer bury their food beneath the bamboo wands. Instead they use two or three wands to baffle the birds and bury their stash to the right or left of their markers to confuse the confounded birds. Don't tell the ravens!

Above the wings of raven the only view is heaven.